302370

DATE DUE		

358 BAK Baker, David
          Peace in space

LA HABRA CITY SCHOOL DISTRICT
Sierra Vista School
500 North Walnut Street
La Habra, California 90631

Peace in Space

Today's World in Space

Peace in Space

By David Baker

Rourke Enterprises, Inc.
Vero Beach, FL 32964

© 1988 Rourke Enterprises, Inc.

All rights reserved. No part of this book may be reproduced or utilized in any form or by any means, electronic or mechanical including photocopying, recording or by any information storage and retrieval system without permission in writing from the publisher.

Library of Congress Cataloging-in-Publication Data

Baker, David, 1944-
  Peace in Space. / David L. Baker.

  p. cm. — (Today's world in space)
  Bibliography: p.
  Includes index.
  Summary: Surveys the development of ballistic missiles and warheads in the United States and the Soviet Union, with an emphasis on the proposed system known as Strategic Defense Initiative.
    1. Strategic Defense Initiative—Juvenile literature.
[1. Strategic Defense Initiative. 2. Ballistics missiles.]
I. Title. II. Series: Baker, David, 1944-
Today's world in space.
UG743.B33 1987   358'.1754--dc19   87-19885
ISBN 0-86592-408-2   CIP
                                                       AC

CONTENTS

1	Shield of Defense	6
2	Rockets and Missiles	8
3	Ways to Stop Rockets	14
4	Beam Weapons	24
5	Weapons for Defense	32
6	How will it Work	36
	Glossary	46
	Index	48

Shield of Defense

For almost thirty years, people all over the world have been threatened by long-range missiles. The United States and the Soviet Union have had nuclear weapons for more than forty years. Before the first long-range missiles were built, nuclear weapons had to be carried in airplanes that took many hours to reach their targets. The bombers had to survive attack from fighter planes and small anti-airplane missiles launched against them. There was no guarantee they would get through.

When the first missiles were built, however, nuclear weapons could be sent to their targets within a few minutes. Fighters and anti-airplane missiles were useless, because the big rockets went far out into space before plunging back into the earth's atmosphere at speeds of more

For many years manned bombers were the only way nuclear weapons could be delivered to their targets. These bombers were vulnerable and could be easily shot down.

By the early 1960s, intercontinental ballistic missiles had been developed and were standing by in underground silos. This is a Minuteman being launched from its silo.

than 15,000 MPH. These weapons were extremely destructive, and there seemed no means of defending towns, cities, and millions of people all across the nation from nuclear blackmail.

Soon, improved missiles were put in submarines and in protected holes in the background, called *silos.* Then missiles seemed to offer some protection against surprise attack. Then improvements were made in the accuracy of missiles, so that weapons in silos were not even safe.

In March, 1983, President Reagan started a research program called the Strategic Defense Initiative, or SDI. He wanted to know if lasers and beam defense guns could stop missiles before they released their devastating warheads. No one knew if it was possible. If it did work, SDI would provide the United States with a screen against attack without having to attack the enemy in response. It would be a truly defensive shield, a peace bubble to protect people.

By the late 1960s large numbers of missile-carrying submarines were at sea to provide a third level of defense.

7

Rockets and Missiles

The first long-range military missile was the V-2, developed by the Germans during the Second World War and used against London and other European cities between 1944 and 1945.

The first ballistic missiles were German V-2 rockets built during World War Two and fired against cities in England, France, and Holland during 1944–1945. They carried a 2,000 pound warhead and flew nearly 200 miles. When the war ended in 1945, military scientists looked for ways to improve the missile's range and strike power. So far, no one knew how to build missiles that could fly several thousand miles with heavy warheads. Atomic weapons were big and heavy. Large bombers could lift only one or two at most.

During the 1950s, scientists in the United States devised ways of reducing the size of atomic warheads. They believed they could make them small enough to fit on the rockets and missiles then being built for the army. These missiles had a range of 1,700 miles, not far enough to reach a potential enemy from the United States. The U.S. Air Force wanted bigger missiles to act as a deterrent. A deterrent is a weapon that prevents an enemy from attacking because he fears being attacked in return and losing more than he might achieve.

The first of these big rockets, an intercontinental ballistic missile (ICBM), was called Atlas. Atlas was ready for use by 1959, and within three years the U.S. Air Force had 142 ready to launch. Atlas had a range of 9,200 miles and carried a single nuclear warhead. Preparing the Atlas for flight took a long time, because it used liquid oxygen and a kerosene fuel. The missile could not be fueled ahead of time, since liquid oxygen boils off at the very low temperature of –297° F.

The Atlas had to be launched from a concrete

Titan 2 was the second intercontinental missile developed by the United States and could carry a massive warhead across several thousand miles.

pad. Because it took several hours to get ready, that made it vulnerable to a suprise attack. The air force had a second missile, Titan, which also had non-storable propellants. Titan was developed into Titan 2, a missile with storable fuel. Titan 2 could be kept ready for launch within about 10 minutes in a protected concrete bunker and raised vertically to the surface for flight.

The U.S. Air Force introduced the Titan 1 during 1961, but deployed only 63 Titan 1s before it began dismantling them for the new Titan 2. By this time, the vulnerable Atlas was on the way out also. No Atlas or Titan 1 remained in service beyond 1964. Instead, the air force introduced the Titan 2, which was soon to be placed in permanent silos and launched through big concrete trap doors. The missile would not have

Development of the Polaris submarine launched ballistic missile led to the Trident, which is now entering service with the U.S. Navy in increasing numbers.

About one thousand Minuteman missiles were deployed by the United States in the 1960s. This missile is now being replaced by Peacekeeper.

Revolutionary War Minutemen, who stood ready to go to war at a minute's notice. Like Titan 2, the Minutemen were put in silos in the ground. By 1967 the air force had 1,000 Minutemen. Within a few years, further developments took place in warhead design. Instead of carrying a single warhead on top of each missile, several nuclear bombs could be carried by a single rocket. Each warhead would fly to a separate target, multiplying the threat from a single launch.

Each warhead is called a *re-entry vehicle*, because it is thrown into space on a large arching path before falling back, or re-entering, through the atmosphere. The rocket motors fire for no more than three to five minutes and then shut down. The missile climbs up to a height of between 500 and 1,000 miles, and then a platform carrying the multiple re-entry vehicles separates from the missiles. Each re-entry vehicle is then separated from the platform in turn.

Peacekeeper will operate from modified Minuteman silos and carry up to ten nuclear warheads on a maneuverable bus.

to be lifted to the surface for launch.

By this time a solid propellant missile, Polaris, had been developed by the U.S. Navy. The Polaris submarine-launched ballistic missile (SLBM) was fitted to vertical launch tubes in 41 submarines. Altogether, a total force of 656 missiles was provided. Meanwhile, the air force wanted a missile that could be launched rapidly. They wanted it to be small, so that they could buy many more than the 54 Titan 2 missiles on operational duty by 1967.

The result was Minuteman, named after the

Missile X

For almost twenty years, the United States has maintained a land-based ICBM force of just over 1,000 rockets carrying more than 2,000 warheads. The Soviet Union matched this in the early 1970s and has not stopped building missiles and warheads since then. Today, the Soviets have about 1,400 missiles and almost 6,500 warheads. In other words, the United States is outnumbered by more than three to one with land-based nuclear re-entry vehicles.

For a long time, missiles were safe inside silos because neither side had very accurate warheads. Now, warheads are so accurate they can get close to silos and blow open the massive

Originally called Missile X, Peacekeeper carries a typical load of warheads on a maneuverable fourth stage designed to allow it to change course after each warhead has been released.

The re-entry vehicles protect the warheads they contain from burning up through friction with the atmosphere. Because they have been dropped off at different, but precisely timed, points in the trajectory, each re-entry vehicle flies to a separate target. This is why missiles with many warheads are said to have multiple independently-targeted re-entry vehicles, or MIRVs.

The Russians followed a similar path, also developing missiles which could be stored in protected silos and MIRVs with many warheads. The Russian rockets were very big. Each of more than 300 SS-18 missiles deployed by the Soviet Union can carry at least 10 MIRV warheads. Using two warheads to destroy each missle silo in the United States, the SS-18 missiles alone could disable 80 percent of the Minuteman force in a suprise attack.

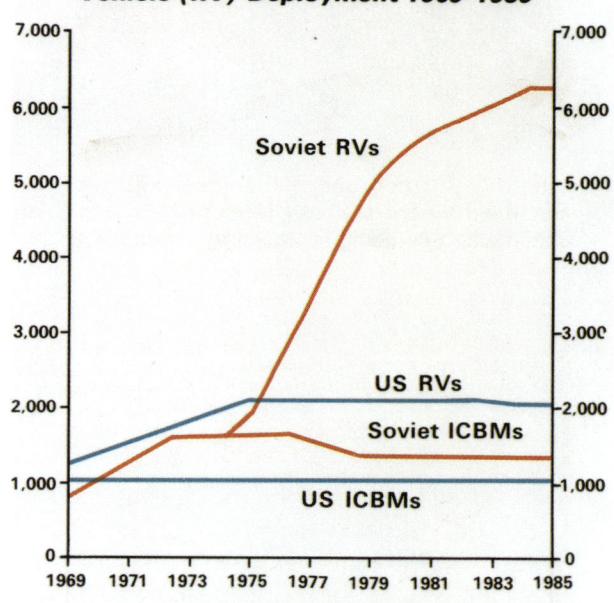

US and Soviet ICBM Launcher and Reentry Vehicle (RV) Deployment 1969–1985

Since peace treaties limiting the size of ballistic missiles were signed in the early 1970s, the Soviets have chosen to expand their force by putting large numbers of re-entry vehicles on each booster, far outpacing the strength of the United States force.

12

concrete doors that cover the firing tubes. The United States would have about 15 minutes advance warning of a missile attack on these silos. Today, the President of the United States would have to decide whether to launch all Minuteman missiles or risk losing them when the warhead fell. The only feasible alternative is to develop a method of stopping the missiles and the warheads before they fall to earth. That is the purpose of the Strategic Defense Initiative.

Missiles launched from silos are controlled by personnel in deep underground command posts. Each missile requires two men to launch it.

Ways to Stop Rockets

For the past forty years, since long-range rockets were first used in war, scientists have been studying ways to shoot them down. Missiles fly at very high speeds. To provide a successful defense against fast missiles, anti-missile rockets must fly at least as fast. Military rockets built to carry warheads, or re-entry vehicles, over great distances are called ballistic missiles. They are launched on long-arching trajectories. Rockets built to carry satellites or spacecraft fly on escape trajectories, which means they escape the gravity of earth. A rocket designed to shoot down a long-range military missile is called an anti-ballistic missile, or ABM.

Scientists have been trying to find an effective anti-ballistic missile ever since the German V-2 rockets were used to bomb targets in 1944–1945. In the 1960s, the threat posed by ICBM rockets with nuclear warheads made the need even more urgent. Rockets were no longer used over relatively short ranges. Now they could hit targets halfway around the world and give little or no warning of their approach.

The flight path, or trajectory, of a typical modern intercontinental ballistic missile has four separate phases. The first includes the boost phase, lasting from launch until the engines burn out. During that time, typically about three minutes, the missile has been

Large radars continually look for incoming warheads and track every object in space in an attempt to get the maximum amount of warning from a surprise attack.

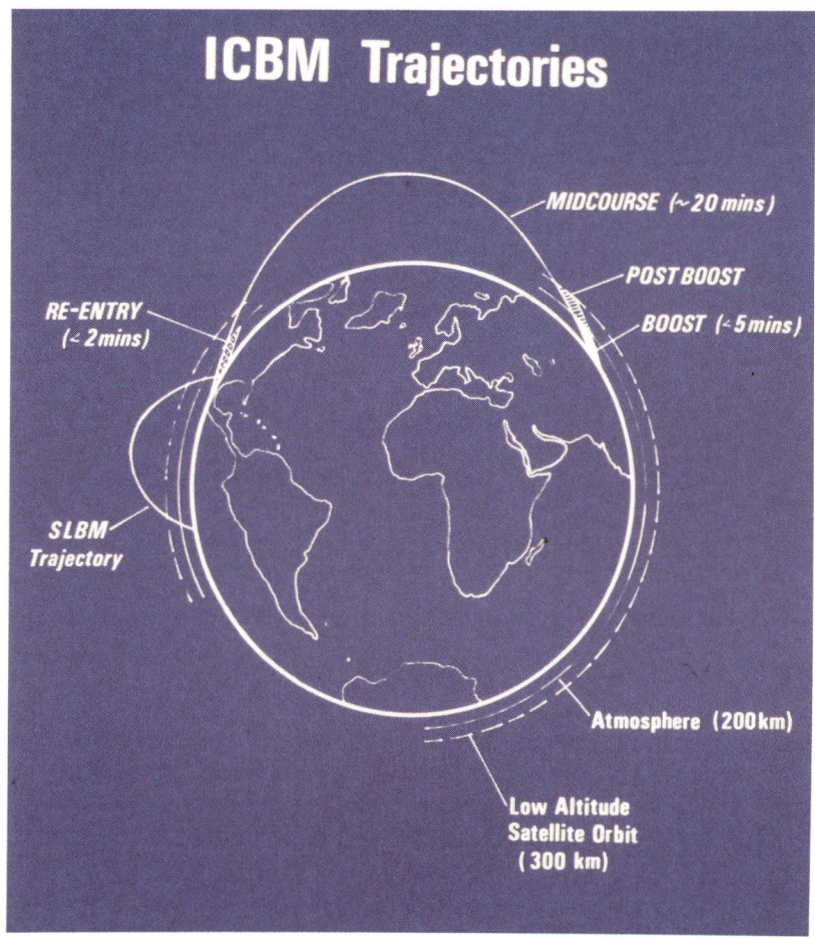

Ballistic missiles fly through four phases between launch and striking their target. These include boost, deployment, mid-course, and terminal phases. Note that distances are given in kilometers, the standard unit of international measurement.

pushed to a speed of about 15,000 MPH. It has reached a height of about 110 miles. During boost phase, the missile gives off hot exhaust from its rocket motors and can be seen from space by satellites watching constantly for signs of launch. It is impossible to hide and can be tracked as it climbs up and through the atmosphere.

The atmosphere gradually decreases with height and extends many hundred of miles from the surface of the earth. For all practical purposes, however, it can be thought to end at about 75 miles. By the time the boost phase is over, the missile is already in space and moving upward on an inclined trajectory. The missile now enters the second phase, where warheads and decoys are released as the missile continues to climb toward the peak height of its trajectory.

In a missile carrying multiple re-entry vehicles (MIRVs), the warheads are fixed to a *bus*, a circular structure on top of the rocket. The bus separates from the rest of the missile, and each re-entry vehicle is then separated from the bus by springs. During launch the warheads are pro-

15

STAGE IV BASELINE DESIGN

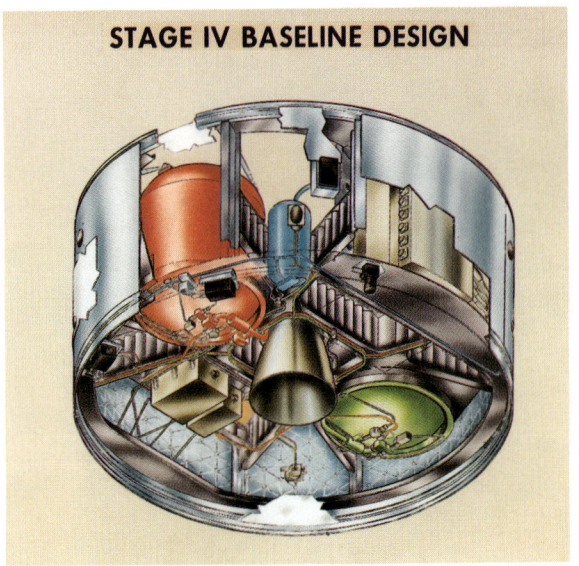

Multiple re-entry vehicles are carried on top a bus designed to maneuver between the release of each warhead. The rocket motor helps to push the entire assembly on its way through space.

tected by a shroud, which must be jettisoned before the warheads can be released. Each time a warhead is released, the bus maneuvers to send them on slightly different trajectories to separate targets on the ground. The bus is moved around by tiny rocket thrusters that fire after a warhead is separated.

This phase is called the deployment phase, because during this time all the warheads, or re-entry vehicles, are deployed. The deployment phase ends when all the warheads have been

The maneuvering bus for Peacekeeper is seen here full size and is surprisingly small for the ten nuclear warheads it can carry.

Technicians measure the clearance between simulated warheads on top of a mounting ring that will be attached to the Peacekeeper maneuvering bus.

separated from the bus. Like the two or three rocket stages that have been dropped off in the first three minutes after launch, the bus is no longer needed and plays no further part in the flight of the re-entry vehicles through space. The deployment phase begins immediately after the boost phase and usually ends less than 11 minutes after launch.

By this time, the re-entry vehicles are approaching the maximum height of their trajectory between the launch site and the target. Peak height is usually around 700 miles above the surface of the earth. As a comparison the shuttle orbits the earth at an altitude of less than 200 miles up. But the peak height of re-entry vehicles has to be high because the targets are probably 6,500 miles away. To achieve such great distances requires a wide trajectory. The greater the trajectory, the higher the peak height must be.

As the re-entry vehicles fly through space, arching over the peak height in their trajectories, they go through what is called the midcourse phase. This phase lasts between 15 and 20 minutes, depending on the distance between the launch silo and the target. The re-entry vehicles are not alone. In addition to releasing up to 14 separate warheads, the bus has also jettisoned up to 100 decoys and electronic targets to mimic warheads.

Decoys are shaped pieces of metal and plastic, aluminized balloons, lengths of metal wire, and other odd bits of junk. These decoys are deliberately put out to fool radar watching

Warheads that get through the main interception phase can be attacked as they are nearing the earth's atmosphere. Defense radars around the perimeter of the United States are vital to maintain a watch on low incoming targets.

for incoming warheads. The radar cannot pick out the real warheads from the decoys. They look very different in size and shape but seem identical to ground radar antenna. This confuses the defenses and means anti-ballistic missiles must attack more than a hundred potential warheads to be sure of hitting the real ones.

When the flight path enters its fourth phase, the decoys are stripped away and only the real warheads remain. The fourth phase is called the terminal phase and lasts only 60 seconds at most. During the terminal phase, the re-entry vehicles slice into the atmosphere at speeds of up to 15,000 MPH and streak to their separate targets. Protected from the heat of re-entry, only the warheads survive. The decoys perish the moment they hit the atmosphere. Only then can the real warheads be counted.

Some warheads maneuver even in the 30 to 60 seconds it takes to re-enter the atmosphere and reach the ground. They are able to dodge and weave, heading for one target then rapidly deflecting to another. Moving at more than 4 miles a second, the warheads can redirect themselves on pre-set commands to cities or missile silos a long way from the targets they

18

seem to be heading for at re-entry. This adds further confusion and complicates defenses.

In the boost phase, the missile is a single target and vulnerable to attack, because it is impossible to hide and highly visible. The missile is difficult to attack, however, because it is over its own territory and around the curvature of the earth's surface. The missile spends only a few minutes in this phase and must be attacked by a weapon capable of firing down upon it.

In the deployment phase, the bus separates and releases up to 100 re-entry vehicles and decoys difficult to attack because they all look like offensive warheads. No heat is produced for sensors to track, as they could with the missile in its boost phase, and the 100 targets seem like

In a simulated test of re-entry vehicles streaking through the atmosphere at 15,000 MPH, six dummy warheads from a Peacekeeper pass through clouds over Kwajalein Missile Range in the Pacific.

cold objects against the cold background of space. An anti-ballistic missile system would have trouble locating all the re-entry vehicles and distinguishing the dangerous warheads from the decoys. Suddenly, by deploying different objects, the single target of the one missile climbing up through the atmosphere has become more than a hundred objects traveling at nearly 4 miles a second.

The mid-course phase carries the warheads and decoys away from friendly areas over to the enemy. In this phase, the warheads and decoys are difficult to track or attack. Even the job of picking out decoys from re-entry vehicles is filled with problems. Some warheads might have been hidden inside balloons appearing to be decoys. Drifting through airless space, the balloon would not be stripped away until it hit the atmosphere in the fourth phase, and the fact that it was not a decoy would not be discovered until literally the last minute. By that time, all anti-missile rockets might already have been used to attack what were thought to be real warheads.

The terminal phase brings special problems, because the re-entry vehicles are moving so fast and might even twist and turn to change course at lightning speed. Any missile attacking an in-

In an attempt to escape attack, the Russians are building more and more missiles capable of being hidden in forests or being driven to concealed launch sites.

Responding to the Soviet lead, the United States Air Force is looking at the miniaturized intercontinental missile called Midgetman, small and with only one or two warheads.

coming warhead would have to reach a greater speed than the re-entry vehicle. If a nuclear weapon was used to blow up the re-entry vehicle, the explosion could very likely destroy towns and cities on the ground. To try to break apart the re-entry vehicle in flight would probably not work. Some warheads are made to detonate if they sense they are being attacked in the terminal phase. This would cause them to explode, no matter what the situation might be.

In a 1960s program called Safeguard, the United States designed two anti-ballistic missiles. The first was Spartan, designed to attack incoming warheads before they reached the atmosphere on re-entry. The second missile, called Sprint, had a super-fast acceleration and

Midgetman would be moved around in a special protected vehicle with the missile lying down in the large horizontal trailer and only erected to a vertical position for launch.

While intercontinental missiles launched from silos give about twenty minutes' warning, missiles launched from submarines off the coast of the United States would cut warning time to between ten and fifteen minutes.

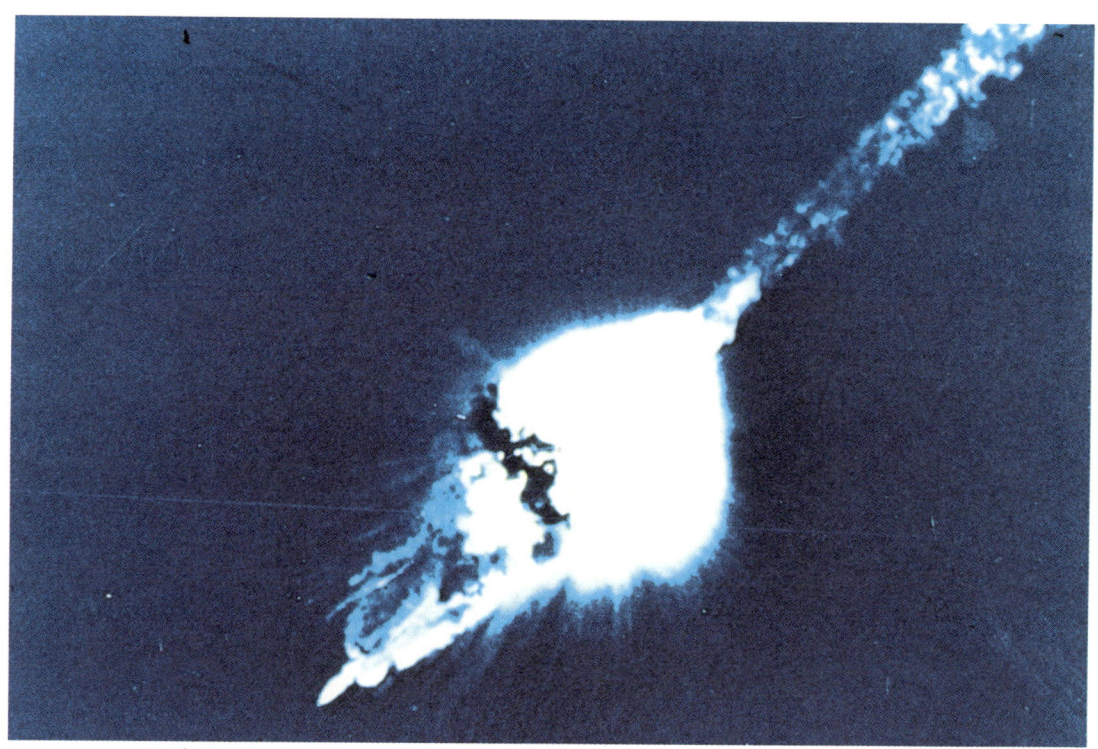

An early ballistic missile defense system like Safeguard was designed to intercept incoming warheads as they neared the atmosphere.

would attack and destroy the remaining warheads that got through. The Russians, too, built up a system which they deployed around Moscow. It is still there today, with 100 ABM launchers in the countryside around the Soviet capital.

The United States chose not to build the Safeguard system, because it was expensive and quickly outdated. When Safeguard was designed, ballistic missiles had just one warhead. When multiple re-entry vehicles were developed in the 1960s, the Spartan and Sprint missiles were not capable of dealing with so many different targets. With a lot of targets to hit, the ABM system would have been a huge network of rockets useful only in the terminal or near-terminal phase. True defense needed a system that would attack the missile before it separated all those elusive re-entry vehicles and decoys.

Beam Weapons

One method of disabling a re-entry vehicle would be to throw a metal net in front of it.

Rocket-propelled weapons designed to attack incoming missiles or re-entry vehicles are called *kinetic weapons.* Kinetic weapons take their name from the use of kinetic energy, the energy or force produced by a moving object. Kinetic weapons are accelerated to great speed for impact with the object they are aimed at. Placed on a collision course by rocket motors, kinetic weapons are any device designed to smash into the target and destroy it. Kinetic weapons are the most familiar type of weapon used for defense.

In fact, throughout time all weapons that have ever been used in war have been kinetic. These include rockets, bombs, and missiles as well as bullets, arrows, and swords. Determining the difference between a defensive weapon and an offensive weapon can sometimes be difficult. Part of the problem is that defensive weapons can cause damage that might be seen as an act of aggression by the enemy. In turn, the enemy might then become more aggressive and expand a local conflict into all-out war, believing that he must attack to prevent himself from being destroyed.

The United States is in such a position. If the President receives word that Soviet missiles are being launched in large numbers, he must quickly decide whether to order all the silo-based ICBMs to be launched in retaliation. But what if it were a false alarm? It would be too late to turn back. The Soviet Union would see a massive attack coming from the United States and launch its own missiles in return. The result would be total, unstoppable nuclear war.

The Strategic Defense Initiative is a way of protecting towns and cities in the United States from unprovoked missile attack. It is the first true defense concept, because it is aimed at weapons themselves and not at people. It is also the first defensive system to be proposed that uses a completely new form of weapon. These new weapons are *laser* guns and beam devices. Striking at the speed of light, they are *directed-energy weapon* devices, or DEW technologies. Unlike kinetic weapons, which travel at several thousand miles an hour, directed energy weapons travel at more than 186,000 miles a second.

In the Homing Overlay experiment, a metal net was packed inside a missile and launched on test.

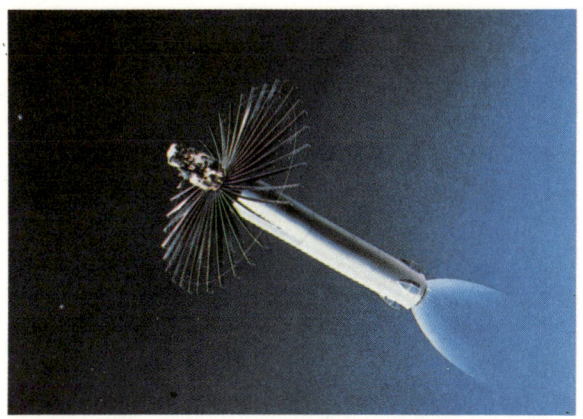

After launch, but still in the boost phase, the net extends. In this test, it successfully disabled the dummy re-entry vehicle.

The following example will put this technology in perspective. Even with modern technology, if a kinetic weapon fired at the moon it could not be made to move at more than 100,000 MPH. It would take that weapon nearly three hours to reach the lunar surface. A laser would take 1.3 seconds to strike its target on the moon. Yet beam weapon technology is extremely difficult and has not yet been proved to work. But if it can work, it will offer a solution that has never before existed: a weapon that cannot under any circumstances be offensive to anything or anyone unless someone else attacks first. The laser or beam weapon can only *stop* rockets being launched in anger or warheads plunging toward towns and cities under attack.

SDI promises to provide a shield without be-

Lasers, developed less than thirty years ago, have evolved into potentially useful anti-missile weapons.

Seen at the Los Alamos National Laboratory, this free-electron laser is designed to operate from powerful ground stations to targets in space.

ing in the least bit offensive to the enemy. After all, what is perceived as an enemy attack might not actually be one.

Complex machines have been built to warn us of attack. They can go wrong and give a false alarm. Likewise, it is not impossible that a missile could be launched by the United States in error. Laser beam technology would enable us to shoot that missile down ourselves before it reached enemy territory, thus preventing a nuclear attack in response.

Laser is a group of letters that abbreviates its technical description: Light Amplification by the Stimulated Emission of Radiation. Its meaning is best illustrated by the example of troops marching in a column. When they approach an iron bridge, the troops break step. Instead of marching in order, they walk normally. Otherwise, they might shatter the bridge if they all march in step, because the shock waves created by all the separate boots will converge. Light is like that also.

Light from a light bulb is a jumbled stream of tiny packets of energy. Like soldiers shuffling

Targets in space might be tracked by this Beam Director, used in tests to develop a system capable of focusing a laser beam on a missile or re-entry vehicle.

On September 6, 1985, an old Titan booster stage was loaded to simulate a Soviet missile rising through the atmosphere in a test designed to demonstrate how a chemical laser could destroy it.

along, there is no order—only a general flow of movement. Tiny packets of light energy, called photons, are brought together in a single beam and passed through filters to remove certain colors. In this way the light is "stimulated" into a coherent flow. Instead of being haphazard, it is focused to a thin beam of energy.

Lasers were developed in the 1960s and since that time have found many uses. Because they have extremely precise direction and speed, they are used to measure great distances. Apollo moon walkers left laser mirrors on the moon so that scientists could measure the exact distance to within inches by reflecting laser light transmitted from earth. Lasers are also used to carry out precise operations on very small parts of the body. Laser surgery is an important part of removing certain cancers or performing operations on eyes.

By striking at the speed of light, a laser can disable a missile by burning a hole in its side or by destroying the electronic systems necessary to keep it on course. The advantage of a laser defense system is that nothing has to be physically propelled to the target. The laser is like a giant torch with a pencil thin beam of highly concentrated energy. It is useless against targets on the ground because lasers designed for use in space would not travel through the atmosphere. It is a purely defensive weapon.

The *particle beam* device is another kind of directed energy weapon scientists are anxious to test. The particle beam has advantages over the laser because it can provide more power and

28

Within seconds of a laser beam shining on it, the simulated Soviet booster rocket is blown to pieces.

operate in areas not suitable for lasers. There are two types of particle beam, one using charged particles and one using particles with no charge. In the nucleus of an atom, the *proton* has a positive charge with the neutron has a negative charge, with one or more electrons which lie in separate shells surrounding the nucleus.

The postively charged (proton) beam is not very effective because it is bent by the earth's magnetic field. The earth is like a giant magnet, and its effect on a proton beam would be much the same. It would bend the beam and make it useless. Scientists are looking at neutral beams made up of atoms stripped of their charge. This allows the beam to remain in a straight line. Particle beam weapons are better suited to working in the atmosphere than lasers because they are not as affected by cloud and rain.

Particle beams are produced in what physicists call *accelerators.* By using accelerators to study complex effects on nuclear particles, scientists gather knowledge applicable not only to the antimissile program but to other peaceful projects too. These benefits have been presented as an im-

This complex device at Los Alamos National Laboratory is designed to help scientists find a way to develop a neutral particle beam weapon capable of destroying electronic circuits in a ballistic missile.

Located in California, not far from San Francisco, is The Lawrence Livermore Laboratory, one of the nation's most important research facilities for laser and particle beam weapons.

portant part of the Strategic Defense Initiative. The SDI Office in the Pentagon has set up projects to help medical science with suitable applications. They promise that industry, too, will benefit by learning of new ways to improve American goods for use at home or as exports. New computers are being developed as a direct result of SDI research. Improvements in computer technology can greatly benefit the electronics industry and help improve the quality and reliability of calculators, computers, and heart pacemakers.

This advanced test particle accelerator is designed to help scientists work on an electron injector for a beam weapon that may find use as a defense device in the 1990s.

Weapons for Defense

Anti-satellite tests employ a rocket propelled impact device launched by an F-15 Eagle, seen here about to drop its load.

Throughout history, deterrence has been based on one country being at least as strong as another, so that if attacked it would be able to inflict the same amount of damage on the aggressor. Ideally, reason will prevent an aggressor from attacking in the first place. The sad truth is that reason has never stopped wars in the past. An aggressor has always emerged who thinks he can beat the odds. The purpose of the Strategic Defense Initiative is to create a screen so that no county can gain a military advantage over another by launching nuclear missiles against the cities and towns in that country. If it can be made to work, SDI might provide countries with a new form of security. No longer would a country try to have the biggest bomb and the largest number of missiles. Instead, it would rest assured that it could prevent missiles being used to threaten it population.

When the Congress of the United States approved research into a ballistic missile screen, they asked scientists to look at several different kinds of weapons. First, the scientists identified the four separate phases of a missile's flight: boost, deployment, mid-course, and terminal. The scientists worked hard to find a means of stopping the missile or its warheads at each one of the four phases, rather than just as the warheads were about to re-enter the atmosphere.

Anti-missile systems fall into the two categories mentioned earlier: directed energy weapons (DEW) and kinetic energy weapons (KEW). The directed energy weapons are space-based lasers, ground-based lasers, and the space-based neutral beam gun. All are beam weapons in one form or another, striking at the speed of light. Kinetic weapons include high-speed rockets based on the ground for attacking targets out in space or inside the atmosphere, small high-speed weapons on the ground or in space designed to strike a missile or re-entry vehicle at great speed, and the *electromagnetic rail gun*.

There has been a lot of work on kinetic weapons, because they promise good results in the near future. Missiles like Spartan and Sprint from the 1960s may have a role in the Strategic Defense Initiative because they could knock out the few remaining re-entry vehicles that get past the other weapons. The United States has developed kinetic energy anti-satellite weapons powered by rocket motors. Launched from converted fighters, these impact weapons take over control after the launcher rocket burns out. Using tiny thrusters, the anti-satellite weapons home in on the heat of the satellite, destroying it by impact.

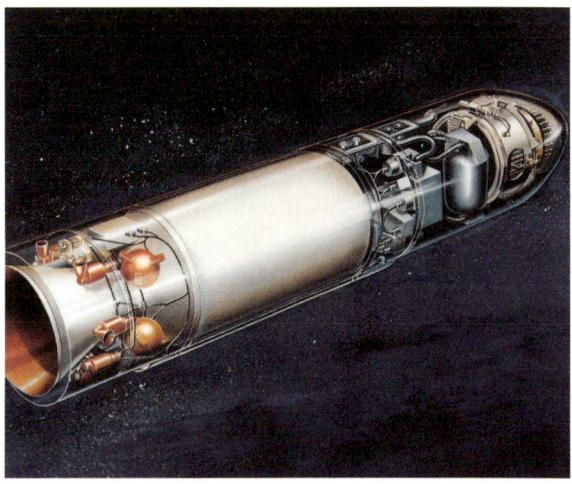

The upper stage of the anti-satellite vehicle is the second stage of the rocket that launched it with the impact head at the front.

This artist's concept shows the impact vehicle as it closes on an obsolete United States satellite during a successful test in September, 1985.

The Soviet Union launches about 100 satellites each year, most of them to control military forces in wartime. If they attacked, the Russians would use these satellites to guide their missiles to targets in the United States. Based in space, high-speed impact projectiles developed from anti-satellite weapons might provide a screen against warheads. More sophisticated versions could be built for use against missiles in the boost phase.

A revolutionary kinetic energy weapon is the electromagnetic rail gun, which accelerates bullets the size of cannon shells along a rail attached to a platform in space. The gun can achieve very high speeds, sending a spray of lethal projectiles several hundred miles to missiles rising through the atmosphere. Knocked off course or destroyed, the missiles would never release their separate warheads. Electromagnetic rail guns could also be used to spray a swarm of re-entry vehicles and decoys. In all phases, kinetic weapons in space offer some hope of destroying the missiles in flight. During the deployment phase they would destroy the warheads when they separate, and in the mid-course phase they would attack them while they drift back toward the atmosphere. Ground-based high-speed rockets can attack the incoming warheads just before they re-enter the atmosphere in the terminal phase.

This electromagnetic launcher has been in testing in San Diego, California, since 1985. Scientists think this special rail gun device might be useful in stopping ballistic missiles in flight.

Known as Checkmate, this rail gun test site became operational in 1985 and has been used to accelerate large bullets to speeds of more than 46,000 MPH.

How Will It Work?

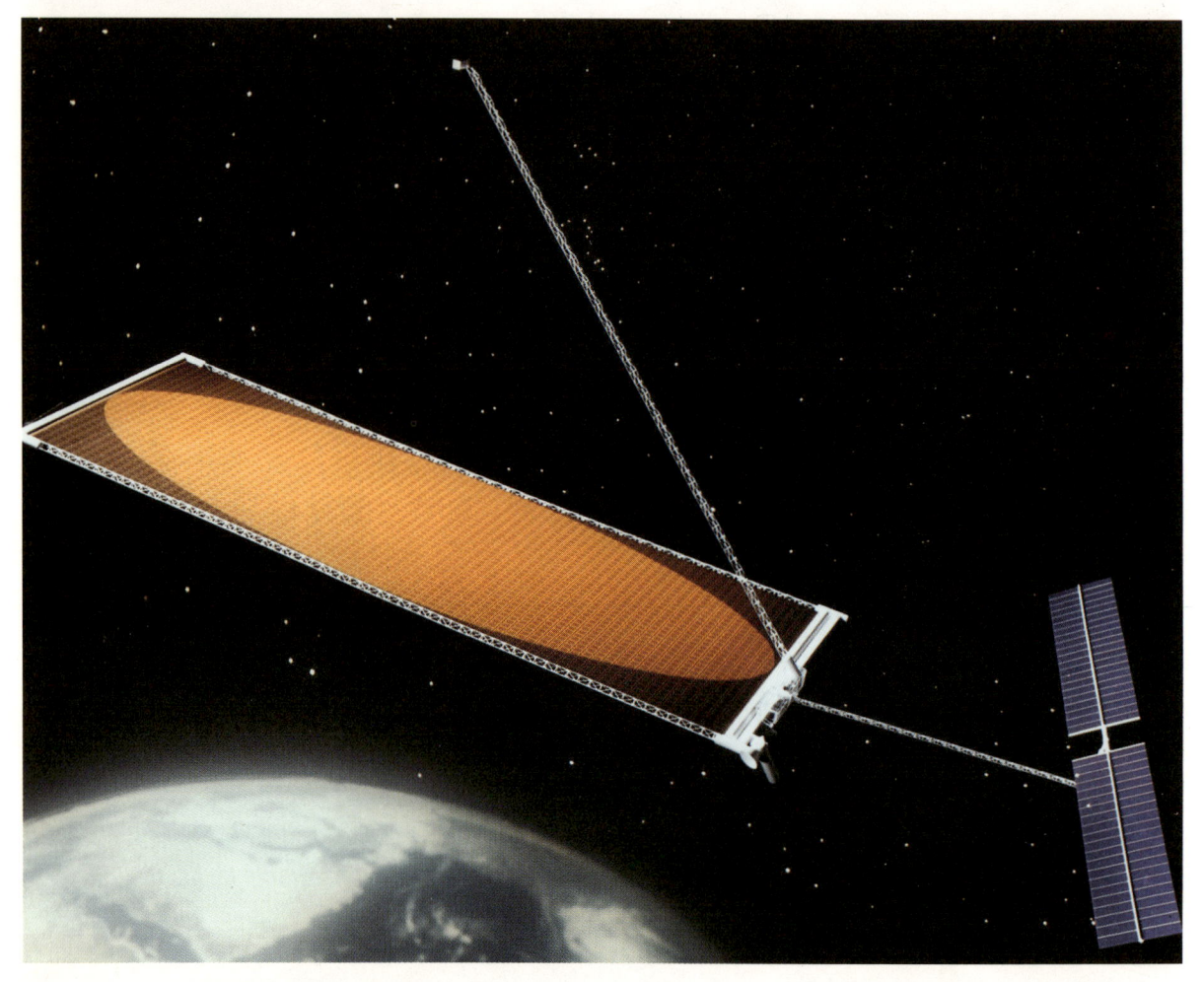

This space-based radar satellite is typical of the kind of system used to warn of enemy attack from warheads hidden among decoys.

The Strategic Defense Initiative is a research program that might last well into the 1990s. Some day it might be possible to build a defensive screen against incoming warheads from ballistic missiles. When a peace bubble is erected, it will use more exotic technology than any other military project. Directed energy weapons, such as lasers, particle beams, and kinetic energy weapons, such as high-speed rockets, projectiles, and rail guns, are just two of four separate kinds of technology vital for a missile screen. The third development is a means of watching for signs of attack. The fourth essential element is a control system to operate the directed and kinetic energy weapons.

Systems for detecting missiles and tracking re-entry vehicles and decoys will be deployed in

This space-based electromagnetic rail gun employs electrical forces rather than chemical propellants to fire projectiles capable of maneuvering accurately to their targets several thousand miles away.

The space-based laser system swings around to intercept ballistic missiles in the boost phase, as the glare from an enemy rocket exhaust looms over the horizon.

space and on the ground. Detectors in space are particularly important, because they can look down and watch for rocket exhausts from land or sea-based missiles. This is called boost surveillance and would involve many satellites in stationary orbit 22,000 miles above the equator. In this orbit satellites keep pace with the earth spinning far below, appearing to remain fixed in space.

Warning of attack would come first via the boost surveillance satellites, which would send detailed information to the ground. The satellites would provide accurate tracking of the missiles and give defense commanders detailed information about the size of the attack and areas from where the missiles were being launched. Very high speed computers would calculate the flight path of each missile in the boost phase and alert the space-based rail guns. Within a couple of minutes the rail guns would start pumping 25,000 MPH guided bullets at the missiles. Perhaps 5 out of 10 missiles would be destroyed before their rocket motors stopped firing.

Still monitoring the situation, surveillance satellites would be tracking the missile buses as they released re-entry vehicles and decoys from the missiles as they tried to climb up through the atmosphere into space. At this point space-based lasers would start firing at the missiles, backing up the kinetic rail gun. With this additional force, 7 out of 10 missiles would be stopped in flight. Meanwhile, neutral particle beam

Opposite page: Gigantic power sources on the ground pump laser energy up to relay mirrors aimed at fighting mirrors directing the laser beams to missiles coming up out of the atmosphere.

38

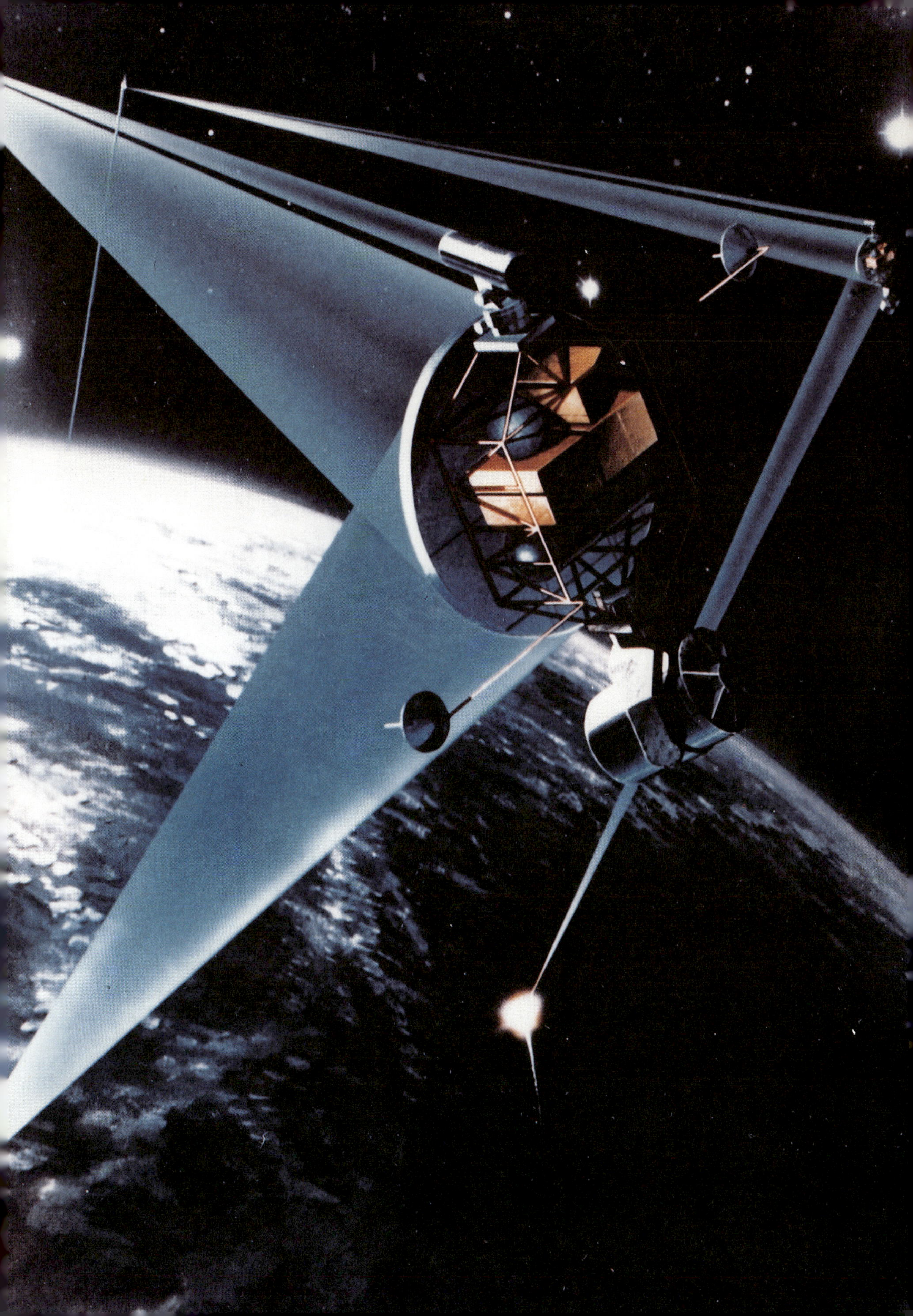

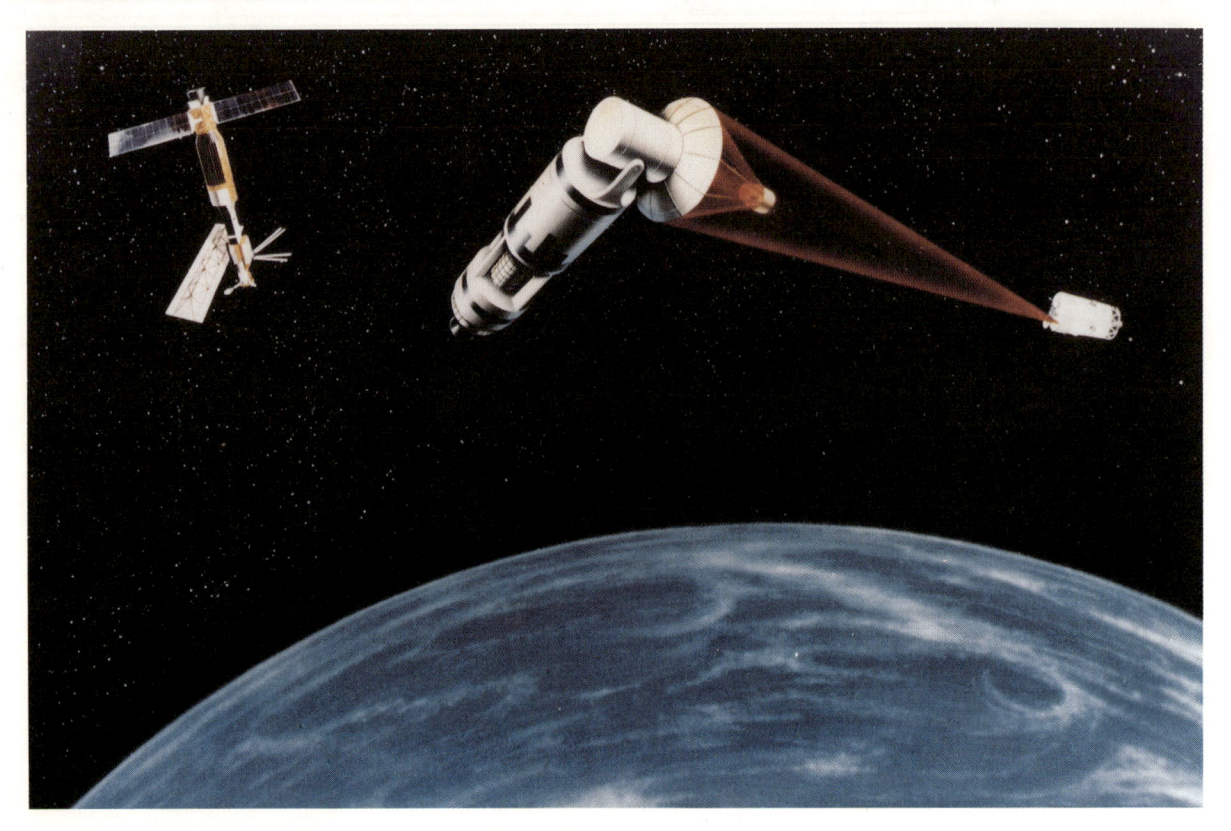

Laser weapons in space direct their energy at maneuvering buses just before separating several warheads and decoys.

weapons would scan the swarms of re-entry vehicles and decoys, trying to sort out which were real and which were dummies, attacking where they could.

Because beam weapons penetrate deep inside the warhead, which is protected by the re-entry vehicle or hidden inside the decoy, they can detect which are real threats and which are false. This gives beam weapons a big advantage over lasers, which can only burn holes in solid objects. the neutral beam probe can provide information about which targets to attack and which to leave alone. Canceling out the decoys reduces the number of targets from about 100 to 10. Also, by probing the re-entry vehicle, the beam destroys the electronics essential to detonating the nuclear warhead. If a warhead exists inside a decoy, the particle weapon will find it.

Ground-based lasers, backing up the rail guns and the space-based lasers, provide enormous power levels to burn holes in rocket bodies and warheads. To reach the missiles several thousand miles around the curvature of the earth, very powerful laser beams generated on the ground would be sent up to relay mirrors in space over the United States. The relay mirrors would send the beams on to fighting mirrors over the Soviet Union. These mirrors would precisely direct the beams on to the missiles and rockets during launch. In this fictional scenario, there are now three forces striving to destroy enemy missiles in the boost phase: rail guns, space based lasers, and ground-based

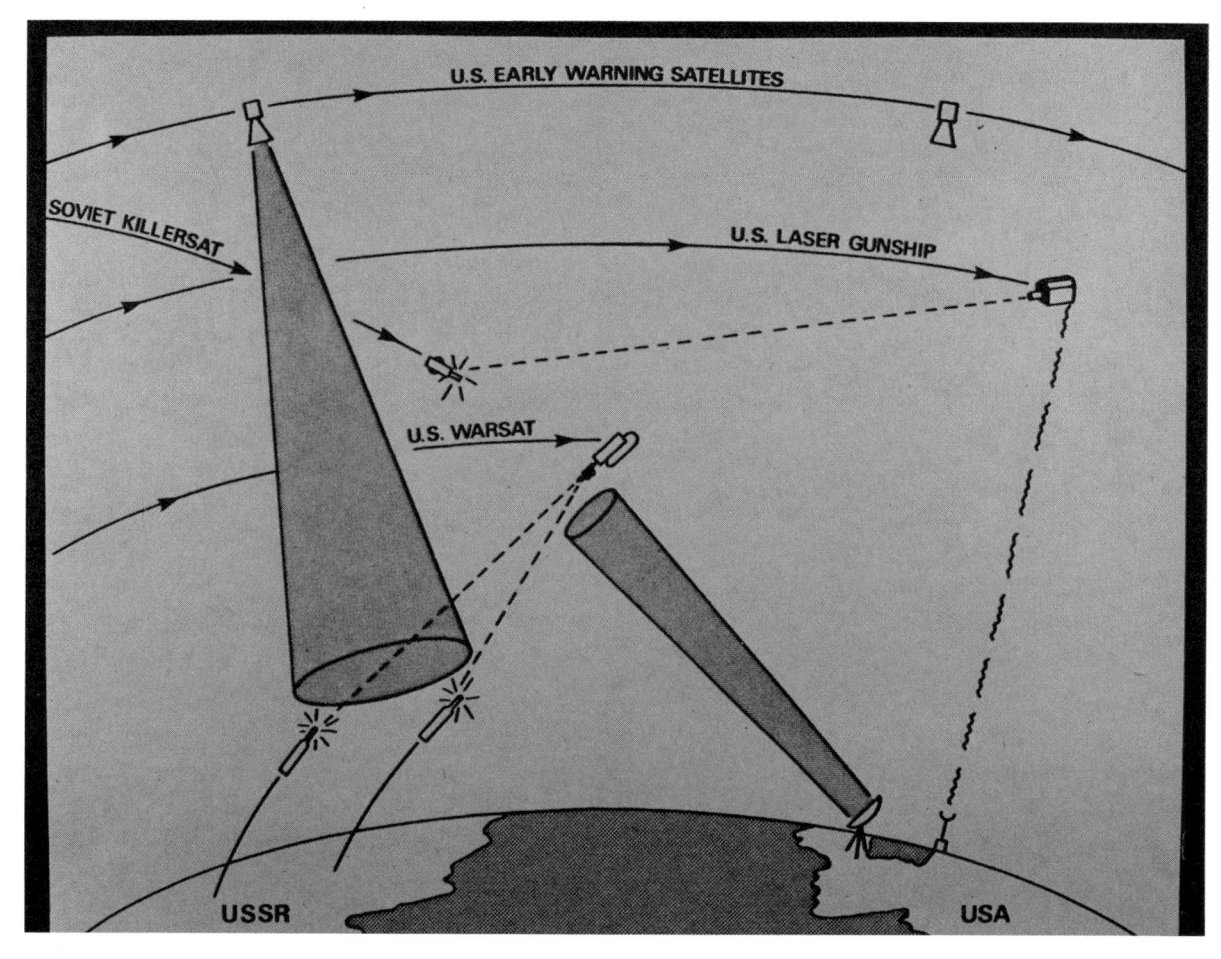

This shows how orbiting warning satellites monitor the progress of Soviet killer-sats attacking United States war-sats knocking out Russian missiles. The killer-sats are attacked by United States laser gun ships patrolling in defense of the missile screen.

lasers bounced off mirrors. Now, only 2 out of 10 missiles slip through.

Another set of ground-based lasers shine beams to fighting mirrors directed against the warheads that survived the rail gun attack during the first wave of missile launches. With the neutral particle beam weapon, two separate systems would now be going for the re-entry vehicles. A third force is added when more space-based lasers back up the ground lasers and the beam weapon. Now there are three separate systems — rail guns, ground lasers, space lasers — attacking the boosters, and three systems — neutral particle beam, ground lasers, and space lasers — burning holes in the separated re-entry bodies.

By now, things would be heating up as more missiles are launched from submarines at sea close to the United States. Today, in peacetime, the Soviets patrol off the Atlantic eastern seaboard and up and down the coast of California with nuclear missiles aimed at military installations. In event of war, they would knock out the command centers first, destroying the

Amid a massive and concentrated attack from silo-launched ballistic missiles, suddenly a swarm of submarine-launched missiles ascends from the frozen wastes of the North Pole, threatening to saturate the defense screen.

computers that control the beam screen. Were that to happen, the submarine missiles would be attacked first by the rail guns and the ground lasers with their fighting mirrors. The mass of silo-launched missiles would begin to overwhelm the defenses. With just 15 minutes to their targets from offshore launch positions, stopping the submarine missiles would be the United States' first priority. The next priority would be stopping the massive SS-18s, each carrying up to 14 separate warheads.

To this point, the defense has been coordinating ground and space-based lasers and beam weapons, but let's assume that the enemy now splits his assault. A double wave attack begins from just off the coast of the United States and from over the North Pole as the big Siberian missile fields unleash their devastating strike force. In space, fighting mirrors are electronically latched to the relay mirrors as massive quantities of power are pumped up from the ground lasers. An almost continuous torrent of beam flashes punch through space, crunching open the tanks of Soviet missiles. More and more missiles fall as the screen is brought up to full power.

By this time, the few remaining warheads that slipped through the triple mid-course screen are tracked as they race for their targets, mainly cities and United States missile silos. The ground-based kinetic weapons begin to swivel around to follow the warheads streaking toward the atmosphere at 15,000 MPH. With lightning acceleration, the first rockets fire off and race for space, destroying the warheads just before they re-enter. Some warheads get through and begin to penetrate. With just thirty seconds to go, super-fast missiles thunder into the atmosphere. The incoming warheads detect they are being attacked and detonate there and then.

They cause no damage to people or property at that height.

In the end, the balance of missiles and rockets are destroyed in different stages of the attack. The fighting mirrors and the space-based laser guns themselves come under fire from anti-satellite weapons. They must not be destroyed, or the screen will go down. Fighters scramble and release anti-anti-satellite weapons to protect the mirrors, rail guns, and beam weapons in space. Those weapons that get through are attacked by squadrons of fighting satellites firing

Low-altitude rail guns hit the submarine launched missiles as they enter space and before they can deploy their warheads.

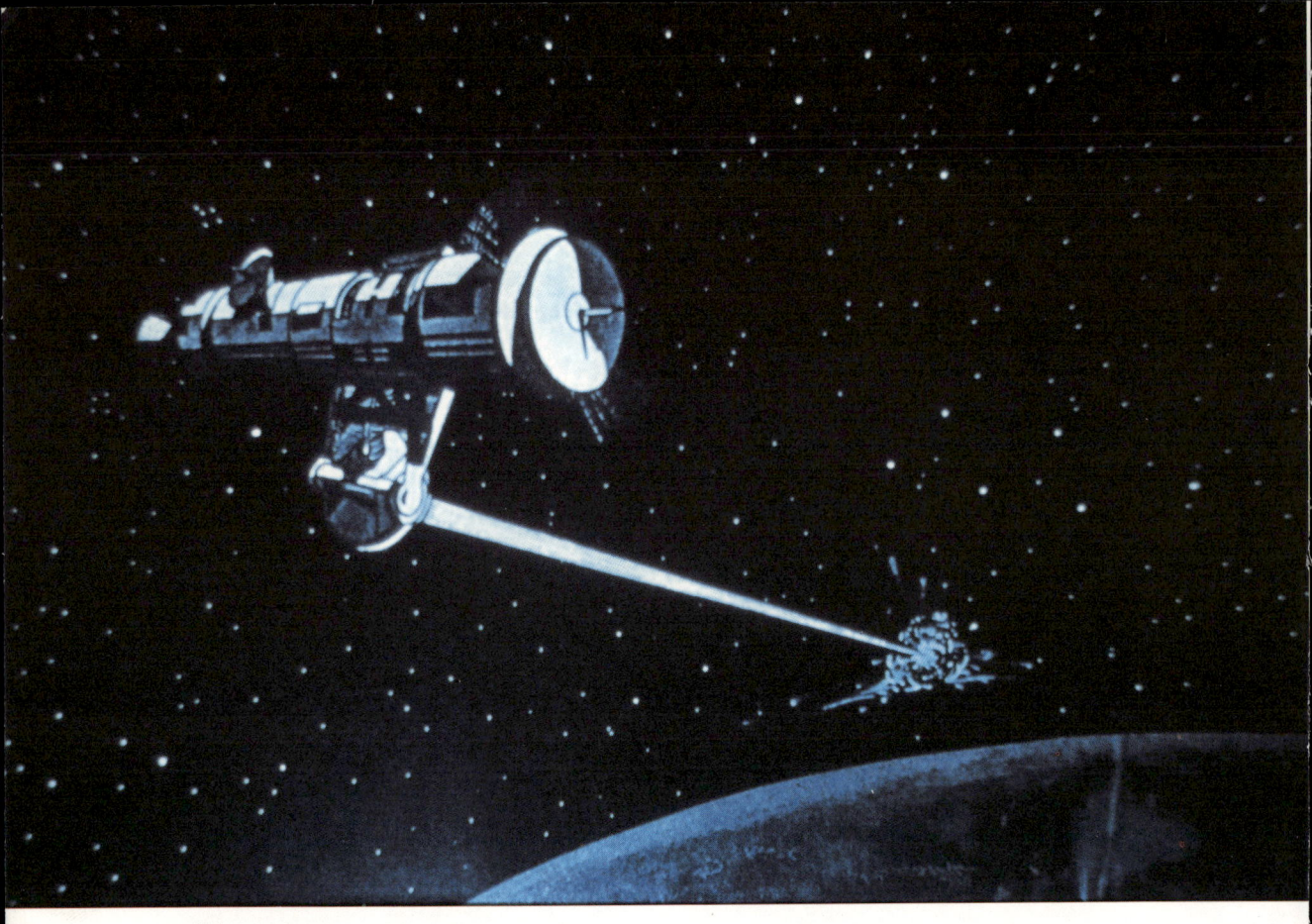

Powerful laser beams go for the decoys and maneuvering buses before they can separate their re-entry vehicles.

high-speed bullets to smash the Soviet anti-satellite rockets. The screen holds up.

All this might never happen. The U.S. might never fall under attack. Likewise, the Strategic Defense Initiative may never be built. The real point is that some sort of defense screen would be a great deterrent to war. With 10,000 warheads on ground and sea-based missiles today, the Russians would never risk losing 9,900 just to get 100 through to their targets. If they did, they would be vulnerable to the more than 8,000 United States warheads in silos and submarines.

Opposite page: The Strategic Defense Initiative is designed to prevent this ever happening for real. It is in fact only a test, carried out over the Pacific in October 1952.

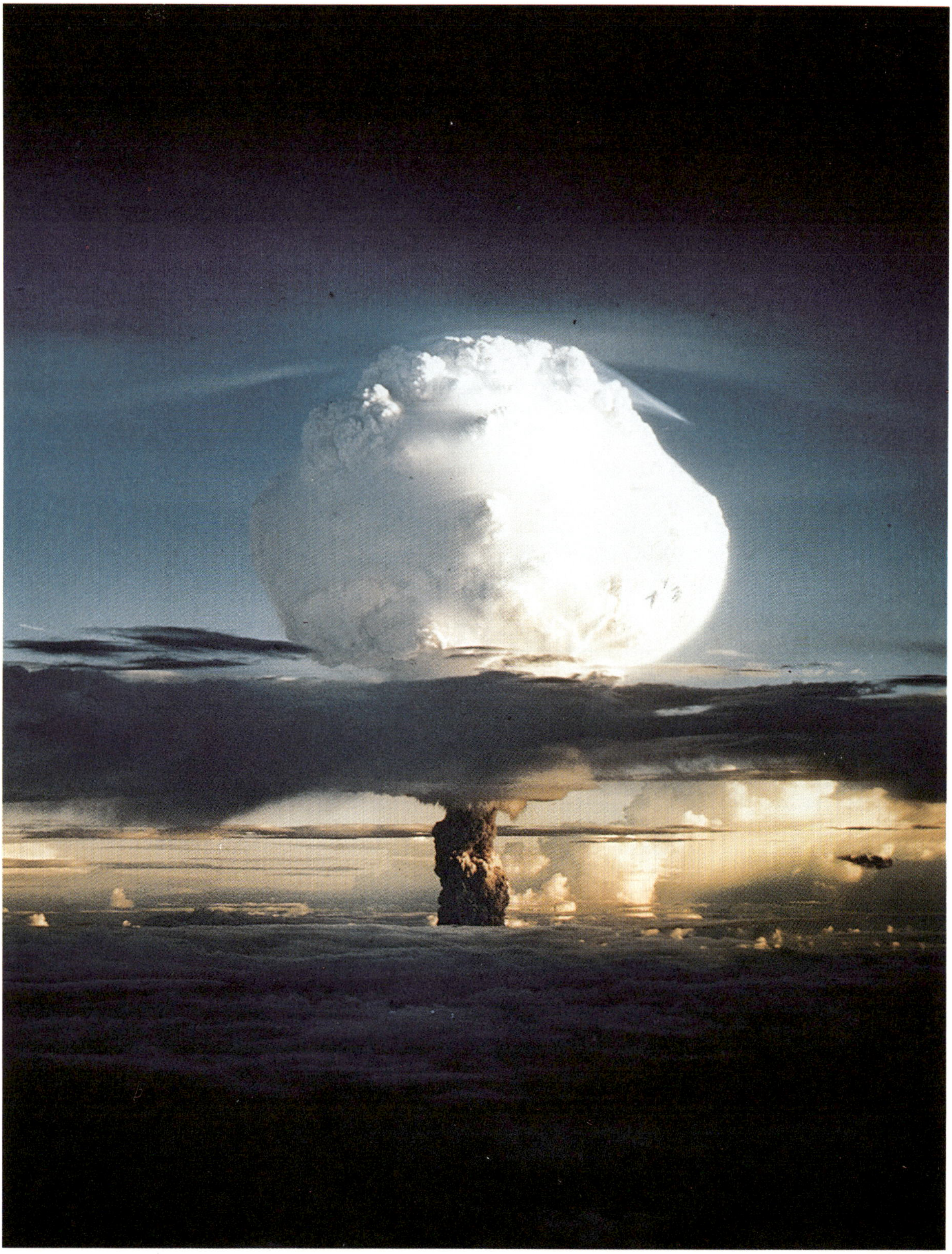

GLOSSARY

Accelerator	A device used by physicists to accelerate atomic particles to very high speeds for research or for some military application like that carried out by a particle beam.
Atlas	The first United States intercontinental ballistic missile, developed by the U.S. Air Force and deployed in the early 1960s, first on ground-based launch pads and then in protected bunkers underground.
Ballistic	Relates to the flight of a projectile after power has been cut off, allowing the object to move under its own momentum and the force of gravity.
Bus	A small rocket-powered platform carrying one or more warheads inside a protective shroud on top of the missile.
Decoys	Any object designed to look like an incoming re-entry vehicle on radar. Decoys may consist of metal or plastic shapes, strips of aluminum, or balloons.
Deterrent	A weapon or combination of weapons that deters an enemy from attacking for fear that he will be destroyed.
Directed energy weapons (DEWS)	Lasers and particle beam weapons designed to strike at the speed of light.
Electromagnetic rail gun	A device using a magnetic rail to accelerate bullets or other projectiles to enormous speed to attack missiles or warheads.
ICBM	InterContinental Ballistic Missile, capable of carrying a nuclear warhead over several thousand miles.
Killersats	Rockets or satellites sent into space for the purpose of destroying the satellites of another country.
Kinetic weapons	Weapons designed to strike or hit another object and disable it by physically smashing some part of it or completely destroying it.
Laser	An abbreviation of the words Light Amplification by Stimulated Emission of Radiation, which means a special device for converting light into an intense narrow beam of energy.
Minuteman	A solid propellant intercontinental ballistic missile developed by the U.S. Air Force for replacing Atlas ICBMs during the 1960s, when the first of up to 1,000 were deployed.
MIRV	Multiple Independently-targeted Re-entry Vehicle. A re-entry vehicle capable of maneuvering inside the atmosphere to dodge and weave through a path of anti-ballistic missiles fired from the ground.
Particle beam	A beam of atomic particles accelerated to the speed of light.
Polaris	A solid propellant submarine-launched ballistic missile developed by the United States Navy during the early 1960s and deployed by sea in as many as 41 submarines during the 1960s and 1970s.
Proton	One of two elementary particles usually found in the nucleus of an atom.

Re-entry Vehicle	A capsule carrying a warhead designed to survive the fierce heat of entry into earth's atmosphere so that the nuclear device inside can be safely delivered to its target.
Safeguard	The system developed in the 1960s to protect United States missile silos from attack, comprising Spartan and Sprint missiles that attack warheads just before and just after they enter the atmosphere.
SDI	The Strategic Defense Initiative, announced by President Reagan in March, 1983. The SDI supports a research program to look at ways of destroying ballistic missiles and warheads in flight.
Silo	A vertical shaft buried in the ground containing a missile that can be fired from inside through open concrete doors normally closed to protect it from exploding nuclear warheads.
Spartan	A very large and extremely fast missile designed to attack warheads before they reached the outer edge of the earth's atmosphere.
Sprint	A super-fast missile designed to attack warheads not destroyed by Spartan.
Titan	The U.S. Air Force intercontinental ballistic missile developed during the early 1960s and developed into a launch vehicle for large military satellites.
Trajectory	The path described by an object moving in air or space, the curved path of a missile.
V-2 rocket	Developed by Germany between 1938 and 1944 as a short-range weapon capable of sending a one ton warhead nearly 200 miles, and used against targets in 1944 and 1945.
Warsats	Sometimes called battle stations, warsats are spacecraft capable of attacking and destroying enemy missiles.

INDEX

Page numbers in *italics* refer to photographs or illustrations.

Anti-ballistic missile (ABM)	14, 20
Atlas	8-9
Beam defense guns	7, 25, 32, 40-43
Boost phase	19, 32, 38, 40
Bus, maneuvering	15-19, *40*, 44
Checkmate	*35*
Decoys	17-20, 23, 36, 40, 44
Deployment phase	19, 32, 34
Directed energy weapons (DEW)	32, 36-38
Fighting mirrors	40, 42, 43
German V-2 rockets	*8*, 14
Homing Overlay experiment	*25*
Intercontinental ballistic missile (ICBM)	8-23, 25
Kinetic energy weapons (KEW)	25-26, 32-35, 36, 43
Laser beam technology	27, 28
Laser weapons	7, 25, *26*, *29*, 30, 32, 36-44
Lawrence Livermore Laboratory	*30*
Los Alamos National Laboratory	27, 30
Manned bombers	6
Mid-course phase	20, 32, 34
Midgetman	*21*
Minuteman	7, *11*, 12, 13
MIRV (multiple independently-targeted re-entry vehicle)	12, 15
Missile X. *See* Peacekeeper	
Neutral particle beam	30, 32, 38, 40, 41
Nuclear war	25
Particle beam device	28, 36
Peacekeeper	*11*, *12*, 17, *19*
Polaris	10, 11
Proton beam	30
Radar	17-18
Railgun, electromagnetic	33-38, 40-43
Relay mirrors	40
Russia. *See* Soviet Union	
Safeguard program	21, 23
Silos	7, 9, 11-13, 22
Soviet Union	12, 20, 21, 23, 25, 34, 41-44
Spartan	21-23, 33
Sprint	21-23, 33
Strategic Defense Initiative (SDI)	7, 13, 24-45
Submarines	7, 22, 41, 42
Terminal phase	20, 32, 34
Titan 1	9
Titan 2	*9*, 11
Trident	*10*
World War II	8

48